Paws and Claws:

Learn About Animal Tracks

by Marianne Lenihan

PEARSON

Scott
Foresman

Editorial Offices: Glenview, Illinois • Parsippany, New Jersey • New York, New York
Sales Offices: Needham, Massachusetts • Duluth, Georgia • Glenview, Illinois
Coppell, Texas • Ontario, California • Mesa, Arizona

Photo locators denoted as follows: Top (T), Center (C), Bottom (B), Left (L), Right (R), Background (Bkgd)

Opener: ©DK Images; 3 ©DK Images; 4 ©DK Images; 7 ©DK Images; 8 (CL, CR) Digital Vision, (BL, TR) ©DK Images; 9 ©DK Images; 10 ©DK Images; 11 (B) Digital Vision, (CR) ©DK Images; 12 ©DK Images

ISBN: 0-328-13358-2

5 6 7 8 9 10 V0G1 14 13 12 11 10 09 08 07

Do you like solving mysteries? Animal tracks are like a mystery. The mystery is figuring out which animal made what track!

Animal tracks give us clues about the animals that made them. Are you ready to learn about animal tracks? Let's go!

Duck tracks

Who tracks animals?

People have tracked animals for many years. People used clues from animal tracks to live in the wild. The dew, a blade of grass, or a budding flower could all give clues about tracks.

We still study animal tracks. Now we study them to learn more about animals.

Bear tracks

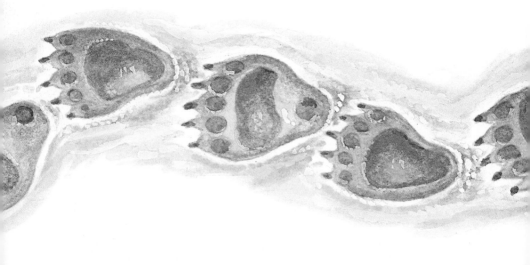

Not so fast!

Before we can identify tracks, we need to know where to look for them. Animal tracks can be found anywhere. Snow, a patch of soft ground, and wet sand make animal tracks easier to see.

Tracks make patterns!

Tracks make patterns. Patterns give us clues about the animal that made the tracks. They can tell us if an animal has two or four feet. They can show whether an animal was walking or running. Patterns can also describe the animal's size.

Track Pattern	How the Animal Walks	Examples
Diagonal Walker	Moves left front foot and right back foot forward at the same time	cats, dogs, horses
Pacer	Moves right front foot and right back foot at the same time	raccoons, opossums, beavers
Hopper	Jumps ahead with back feet	rabbits, squirrels
Bounder	Moves both front feet forward. Then quickly brings up back feet next to front feet	weasels, minks

Not all tracks look the same.

A track's shape gives us many clues. Some tracks show the number of toes an animal has. Other tracks show what kind of hooves an animal has. Some animals leave trails instead of tracks. This snake makes tail and belly trails.

Snake trail

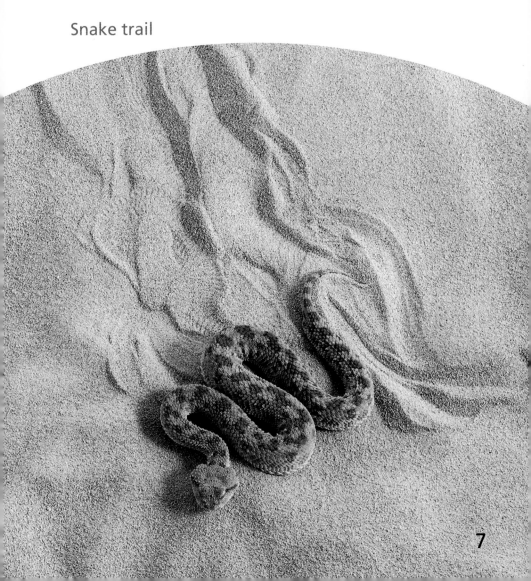

Four Toes All Around

Many animal tracks show four toes on both the front and back feet. Cats, dogs, and rabbits make these kinds of tracks. Cat prints are special. Cats pull in their claws when they walk or run. Dogs and rabbits keep their claws out.

Cat track

Dog print

Four Up Front and Five in Back

Mice, chipmunks, and squirrels are all rodents. Rodents have four toes on their front feet. They have five toes on their back feet. Rodent tracks also have claw marks. Rodents' back feet leave long prints that are easy to see.

Squirrel tracks

Five and Five

Badgers, beavers, raccoons, and skunks belong to the same family. Each of these animals has four feet. Each foot has five toes.

The prints from a raccoon's front paws look like a human child's handprint. Beavers' back feet are webbed. They make unique tracks.

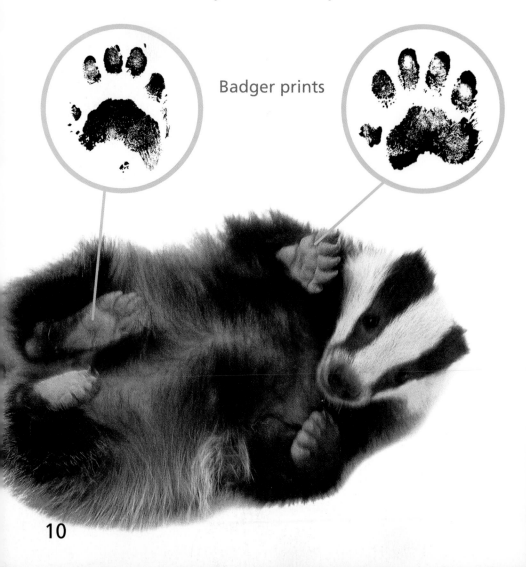

Badger prints

Different from the Rest

If you live near open fields then you might have seen deer. Deer, elk, and sheep are cloven hoofed. This means that their hoofs are split. Deer also have two toes, called dew claws. These toes are behind each foot's hoof.

Sheep track

It's for the birds!

Birds hop and walk. Bird tracks are easy to tell from other kinds of animal tracks.

Some animals don't leave tracks. Fireflies flutter, for example. They don't leave tracks that we can easily see.

You've now learned about many different animal tracks. So get a notepad, and go check some out!

Crow track